To *After That* (Toaf)

Renee Gladman

atelos

31

ISBN: 978-1-891190-31-5
First edition, first printing

Ŧ Atelos

A Project of Hip's Road
Editors: Lyn Hejinian & Travis Ortiz
Text Design and Typesetting: Travis Ortiz
Cover Design and Artwork: Ree Katrak
Cover image, Monotype, *As Long as I Remember*
        Used by permission of the artist.

Toaf

"Let me see it," as strange as this sounds, was my first thought when I returned home this evening. Hours before—having printed the last page of the manuscript and prepared to flee the house—I had written "After That: a novella" across the title page, then I ran outside. When I was about a block from home I turned around and came back. I pulled the manuscript out again—a crisp stack of ninety-seven very white, very smooth pages—and scribbled in black ink "When I was a poet" just under the title to qualify things. I changed my outfit, adding a new, more versatile layer (a hooded sweatshirt), and left my house decidedly. I was outside; the relief I felt was tremendous.

In the summer of 1998, I set out to write a book that when completed would weigh three pounds. I did not know what else I wanted. It might even have been 1999 that I started the book. I have nothing conclusive to lock its inception in place. This book would concern my favorite subject—the problem of the person in time and space—and would flow from the farthest left margin to the farthest right, the way novels did in bookstores. But its story—the exact parameters of it—I did not deem necessary to know right then, as this was my first novel, and would be a ghost book.

Luswage Amini, the great Ravickian novelist, once conferred to an interviewer: the first novel will be given to you from the remains of some other's long lost project. Despite how this sounds—to my ears, a bit foreboding and overwrought—I was not afraid of the inheritance. It was not unlike the moment one finally opened one's mouth—past the babbling stage of life—to speak. That language I emitted, those many years ago, though it was peppered with resistance, it was somebody else's language. It was even somebody else's resistance. So I addressed the blank pages of my journal, place where I was to write the first draft of the book, as one would the top half of the receiver to a telephone. That is, I put my ear to the left side of the journal and transcribed on the right.

I began the book, "For as long as I can remember…" and wrote steadily for any hour. Something odd was happening to my life, which nearly distracted me from my purpose. It seemed that the time elapsing inside the narrative I was writing did not match that which elapsed outside, in that place where I sat. And though this did not affect me physically, it made me extremely conscious of everything falling away into folds. I wrote until I landed on the words, "Where the heat settles and the water is hot," and closed the journal without further incident. I had six pages of apparition between the leather covers that bound the book in my hands, and that seemed to be enough.

As I wanted to get across in my novella, I lived in a city of rough surfaces that left patterns on you. Where they marked you depended on how closely you embraced them. Along the sides of my body (moving vertically) and on both sides of my hands (these moving every-which-way) were scratched permanently the lines to my story of that city. I think on my body the surface of every building is imprinted. And it is not just that I loved to touch concrete, I sought to sit on it as well. It was my custom to nest on cemented squares, in patches of sun, on the avenues of downtown. Well, now I remember that, at the very least, my book would be about concrete.

The fact of having written six pages previous to now sitting at a table over coffee made everything I thought subsequently glimmer. Everything I thought seemed to belong in the book. I wrote furiously on napkins, no choice without my journal, which I had left at home (I could have asked someone for paper, but I didn't want to go through society to get to my work, plus I liked the picture: black girl scrawling desperately on napkin upon napkin. What that must have looked like. What a lone black girl might be thinking.) I was deeply silent those minutes. It was more than that I did not talk to anyone or that I held myself (other than my hand and my arm) still, it was that I did not breathe, my blood did not flow. I wanted to connect the six pages to these eight or ten napkins, and it seemed the only way for that to happen was to diminish as a person, to be lifeless for that long moment. In those minutes, I begged the napkins to relate themselves to the gestures I had already made. It had happened before that something I'd thought was a continuance to a piece of writing I'd left at home was, when I had brought the two together, another thing entirely.

I stopped writing after napkin nineteen and left that café. I had never walked through the city with so much ephemeron on hand. I mean napkins are ephemera no matter what is written on them. I walked along South Street with, I imagine, an odd expression on my face, probably smiling, probably snapping my fingers. When later that night I copied the new text into my journal, I was thrilled to find that I had amassed fifteen pages. One page short of my previous novel attempts, and these pages I knew were only the beginning.

The impulse to write woke me the next morning. But how could I slow this down? I knew the experience had to be different. To write something completely unlike anything I had written before, I would have to alter my process. I could not pour into the page, as was my instinct. However, controlling myself proved to be impossible. At the end of that first hour of writing, I had invented a whole world. There was a film, a day of tasks, and a cell phone.

For years since I have tried to put a name to the mood that descends upon me after such repeated bursts of writing. It is exhilarating to be drenched in this way, but at the same time frustrating, not unlike excessive masturbation, where instead of becoming more relaxed the more you come, you find yourself weary and hungrier. I was disappointed that I could not write as a novelist, with plans and foresight, and that I wrote impulsively like a poet. I wrote with obsession, bent over my journal, "coming" and chastising myself for coming.

It soon became obvious that parts of the book—perhaps even the overall project of the book—were intent on working out the idea of sequence. It appeared that the notion of events moving along a system of succession, one like time (although there are other such systems), was a natural preoccupation for a student living in an urban location. This is not how I thought of myself then, but seems all right to say today. Then, the designation "student," much less "graduate student," was difficult to occupy when your school stood on an ordinary city block, consisting of two buildings that faced each other from opposite sides of the street, and roll was never called. I had been a student from 1989 to 1993, a college student, now I was a poet. But I was an extremely outdoor poet with a lot of things to do. I lived with my dog Eva. The books in all the stores were calling me. I had to get my coffee. My burritos. I had to sit on this step and lounge on that piece of grass. The lifestyle I adapted required filling up a day with pursuit and leisure, but at such a tempo it was difficult to say which was which.

And writing took place somewhere in between. Writing was about returning home "half the person" and looking into the space of language for a refill. But not just to put back what the outside had taken, also to add some new information. To graft that day's terrain onto the previously accumulated—so to make a great big map. In those days it did seem possible to incorporate life.

The city in which I lived during the writing of the novella *After That* was concrete and exhausting, but also special, beautiful. On many of the streets I did not know the language. The corner stores seemed bursting with fruit. In fact, they *were* bursting, spilling out onto sidewalks, protected from the sun by tarps. Their labels bore prices, but rarely names. To buy them, you had to make a clown of the body, using your hands and feet to indicate shapes and color. I traversed that concrete city with both hands: one stretched toward oncoming traffic, the other bringing snacks to my lips. Crossing the street was atrocious.

Yet I would wake and write this novel and I would stay up late and write it. But I was not alone; there was a lover, who knew me. I brought her into the novella and I named her Frog. Today she is called Chubby. It was to her, six years later, that I dedicated the book. I wrote: For Chubby, the first to come. That is to say, the first to be moved to masturbate upon finishing it, which apparently she did on her bed, in a swath of sun.

The book I was writing was scored in the key of leisure, in the way I had leisure as a student. But at no time in the year of that first draft did I actually have leisure. Then, I explained the discrepancy to myself as "There is fiction and then again there is life." But I knew it was ridiculous and even trite to think in such a way. Because, before I had the time to complete such a thought, the one had already become the other. This is another thing I wanted to say in the novella *After That.*

One morning, an unsettling thought came to me. I realized (though without knowing how to protect myself from this awareness) that the events I was so enthusiastically unfolding in my new novel were not embellishments from my life, as I had all the while been assuming, but out-and-out lies. There was nothing true about them. At the time of this revelation,

I had not yet—to myself or anyone else—applied the word "fiction" to my writing (only to my living, as I have just explained). It would take two more years before I could utter such a relation. However, the words "novella" and "novel," I had no problem with. "I'm writing a novel," I said constantly to anyone who would hear me, and the misnomer received no extraordinary attention.

Frog was proud to be associated with a woman writing a novel. I think more so than she was proud to be with a woman composing poems. The draw was longevity: she knew we had something to talk about for at least two years, and that the more we talked about it the more she could say. She was becoming an expert on what I should and should not do as a former poet writing her first novel. She was full of advice: "You've got to read this book on time by J. Fraser. It's all about infrastructure," or "You've got to be more linear here. It's not poetry." I wanted to read that book, I wanted to stay in line. But, I never did. I had forgotten to.

Nor did I cease making the world of AT out of what must have been nothing other than instinct. I knew nothing. Six years later, I think all is still unknown.

In 1998, I submitted a manuscript to a small press; the manuscript consisted of four almost-novels. My first impulse was to name the book *Four*, a gesture that I thought might encourage the reader to trust me. That is, Renee Gladman, not to be confused with my narrators, who were completely unworthy of trust. *Four* would state what the book contained. Four personas. Four places. Four narrative strands. Four could-have-been-novels-had-I-the-capability. I submitted the book, then awoke the next day and changed the title to *Juice*. The typography on the cover—once designed and produced—renamed it *Juice Juice*, though few people noticed this. I have tried not to complain.

I submitted this book and a few days later lunged addictively into the new one, a definite novella. I am three-quarters sure that this is what I did. For the fact that I did not keep a diary at this time (at least I have not found one) there has been some confusion as to whether I began this project in the summer of 1998 or that of 1999. It being late winter of 2004, one would think it not too difficult to differentiate one year from the other, when those years were not so long ago. However, my memory clouds over in certain places. While it is certain that from 1994-1996 I ate pasta and garlic every night of the week, and from 1996-1997 I began to integrate pasta and garlic with an occasional meal of lentils, rice, and garlic, then from 1997-1999 eating lentils, rice, and garlic exclusively, it is much less certain the year in which I began this book. I have combed the annals of my mind and even the minds of my friends, and nothing is certain.

But I did begin this book and I did write and write it.

The way one carries one's productivity around in urban space is joyous: everything you experience from that moment—the moment you realize that you've really created something—feels good. That joy lasts as long as your walk through the city, and dissolves when you return home to your work, to how far there is left to go with it.

One day, after I had typed in all the pages from my journal, the idea occurred to me to make chapter breaks. I made thirteen. The next day I erased the chapter breaks and added a row of asterisks to separate one part of the narrative from its subsequent part. Three days later I put the breaks back, but changed the font of the chapter numbers. I remember this perfectly. I also experimented with the margins. The manuscript bulged and shrank from thirty pages to forty-five to fifteen depending on how wide was the frame I wished to place around it. I have always been a white-space writer.

Plus, Frog had said she would bake me a pie were I to reach page forty-five (an arbitrary goal I had set for myself) by the weekend. She was hoping to have my undivided attention for a trip to the beach. The pie was to encourage me to write more, faster. On Thursday, when it appeared that I was not going to make it, that I would have to write into the weekend, I became anxious. Yet, I did not increase the font size of the text. That would have made me feel cheap. But I did make two-and-a-half-inch margins all around, pushing the page total to forty-six. I was thrilled, and then shortly after, full of guilt. I gave Frog the weekend she wanted, but when I returned to work that Monday morning, I re-adjusted the margins. I settled on thirty-eight.

I said I have always been a white-space writer. So far I have not suffered because of it.

I am trying to convince my current publisher that novelists have long wrapped their prose with that dense emptiness. As soon as I get through to them (I've been calling for days), I tend to provide them with a list of names. Nathalie Sarraute, renowned French experimentalist, will rank prominently on my list, not to mention Luswage Amini. And it is not to fatten our books—though I certainly enjoy that consequence—that we surround our texts so liberally. But to communicate to the reader that something is missing, that the text before you is a partial, a shaving from some whole, somewhere else. Unfortunately, I'll need to have an answer ready as to where that "else" is. Right now, I am not prepared to say.

That city, that for lack of a better word *housed* my novella, remained—for the duration of the first draft—faithful to me. By faith, I mean that it kept its light on: I could see it as I had come to love it months after it no longer was itself. Thanks to the economic boom of the late nineties. The temperate climate kept me calm, but everyday I mourned the displacement of the city's people. I saw my favorite streets overcome: apartment buildings, having stood a hundred years, demolished in a day to erect lofts, holes-in-the-walls restructured into boutiques, and new money-laden citizens crowding the sidewalks. Years before, it was the bank receipts people left behind at ATM machines, the bold disclosures of wealth, that alerted me to what was ahead. Nobody with three hundred dollars or less in the bank ever left those slips behind. The slips signaled in 1996 that something was going wrong. But it was not until 1999 that you felt the full brunt of it.

In the fall of 1997, I moved into a two-bedroom flat, just up the street from my previous residence, though here everything was different: now I had one roommate instead of three, which meant I could occupy the living space less anonymously.

The reason I, at times, experience certainty that I started this book in the summer of 1998 is that through the window of this new bedroom I saw my first concrete tree. I was struck by what I thought was an anomaly, until I began seeing this type of tree all over that unique city. Within the first few sentences of the novella *After That*, you will find, "The concrete tree outside my window," written quite simply. Years later I would have to re-write that passage, as too many people unfamiliar with the concept (concrete tree) worried over its "incongruous" presence. A few months ago, I addressed this concern by changing the text to "The trees outside my window are the first in a series of architectural leaps intended to beautify this city—these saplings 'protected' by cylindrical holds of concrete." To those of you who also lived in this great cement city, I apologize for such an overt description. But, there are certain things one cannot understand if one has never seen them. For instance, it never snowed in my previous city, the city of the novella. Yet, today it is late March in my new city, and flurries blow past the window. I have called Chubby to tell her this and she sputters, "What? What?" wrapping her mind around the concept.

This is what you do when you are editing, isn't it? You move text around; you delete something that does not have the anticipated effect on your trial reader; you write down somewhere that you have deleted that thing, then you put a question mark beside it. How many times have I been thrown into confusion when explaining to someone the cuts I've made—that person being different from the trial reader—and that person has responded with a violent shake of the head, pressing the point, "I totally understand that. Put it back in." The number of times I have done that matches the number of times I have run to a nearby park, thrown myself on a bench, and fallen over with my head in my lap, my hands scraping the ground, with the smallest of smiles on my face. Confusion is a gift, I have always thought. That is the reason for the smile. Similarly, when I am in the midst of an overwhelming sadness—those moods that have no identifiable cause—I begin to marvel over the ability to have such feelings. I write something down, usually on a loose sheet of paper, thinking the feelings too fleeting for my diary, and give that smile again—buried in the typical frown of sadness—because what I've written is beyond me. Eventually one comes to know what belongs in a book one is writing and what does not. And eventually one changes one's mind on all of this.

It was 1998 when began the true disfigurement of public space by the ever-proliferating "private conversation." I am talking about the advent of the cell phone. It did not enter my life sensibly.

In chapter four of the novella *After That*, I tried to illustrate the degree to which this change disturbed me. Of course, now I have to speak tenderly of it, as this disturbance has become a way of life. But, at the time, I bemoaned it bitterly, using the disgust to fuel my writing. This "inspiration"—annoying as it was—led me to an understanding: the scope of a narrative work is determined by two opposing intensities. They are propulsion and repulsion. I would use the latter to do what all those years (well, for the two that I had been writing prose) I had failed to do: amass pages; write one continuous book. And with the former, I would explore the mechanics of time.

I should slow down. This has always been my problem. I am talking about the thing as if it floats here before us. Unfortunately, it does not. In fact, I do not know where it floats.

Perhaps what is needed is that I show the reader what I have meant by "the novella *After That*"; it was not just an idea. The pages I wrote were real. That I performed chapter four in a tiny bar in the city of ghosts proves it. And if not, I place it, in its entirety, below:

Charlotte lived down the hall in 3C. I saw her with her cell phone on the morning I was to see Anna's film; she was in my apartment. I let her in to borrow a third cup of sugar, then left her to make her way out while I went to take a shower. When I had finished, I found her in my kitchen making waffles and talking to herself with the palm of her hand against her ear. Was she on the phone? In such awkward situations, one expects the intruder to ask the person with whom she is speaking to hold on, but Charlotte, so involved in her conversation, only waved when I walked in.

I thought, how is it that she is making waffles in my kitchen when I have somewhere to go?

It was obvious that she was having trouble when she started to scream, but she was heating up the waffle iron, too. She was screaming, then dipping her index finger in batter, saying, "No, fuck you!" then smacking her lips over batter.

Her actions really got to me. I had to take some space. I ran into the living room, sat in my favorite chair, and reclined to think things over. There is Charlotte in my kitchen, shouting and making waffles. She has a cell phone. Then, I thought, Oh! Is she dressed? I got up and sneaked around the corner... puzzled...why was she wearing a linen suit and still smacking that waffle batter?

I must have sat there for over an hour reeling the sequence over in my mind: Quiet Charlotte, a good neighbor, is in my house making (me?) waffles in a linen suit and yelling at "Tom!" on her cell phone. Other than "Can I borrow some brown sugar?" she had not said a word to me.

Suddenly, she yelled "Bye!"—I thought into the phone—but after another hour of wondering, I grew curious about the silence. I walked into the kitchen, swelled with apprehension, unfamiliar with my surroundings (as though this were not my home). There was a white square plate that I had never seen before on my dining table, a peach washcloth, which normally hung near the bathroom sink, folded neatly beside the plate, and a perfectly cooked waffle buried in butter on the plate.

My waffle iron was gone. The cell phone was propped against the milk next to the butter. She had wiped the counters clean—scoured them, really. I did not recognize my kitchen. I knew it was my kitchen because my towel from that morning's shower was draped across the opposite chair.

I recognized the sun streaming through the window.

Clearly this scene builds and culminates with expedience (I have never been big on elaboration), but I think it does enough to get across what is wrong with cell phone users. That someone would think the contraption equaled if not surpassed the worth of a waffle iron is quite ridiculous. In 1998, I thought that would be all I needed to produce the repulsion side of my equation. Movement would commence at the onset of empathy, especially, once the narrator left her house, and the phone (which she brought with her) began to ring.

Out of the blue, in the fall of 2000, Chubby purchased her first cell phone. I began to worry. Many of my acquaintances had already been swept up in the melee. But Chubby was a radical, not only a radical but also a reactionary. Had I only recorded her early rages against the mobile phone, against those who indulged it publicly, I might have been able to keep her. That day she held it in the palm of her hand, cupped to the side of her head, like a baby pillow (baby, because the thing was so small), with her eyes sealed tight. It was disturbing, their immediate intimacy.

In those early days, I was flawlessly resistant; I even tried to make it an issue about colored versus white, saying it was another thing that white people did that irritated me. But anyone living in the United States, or any other place in the world with access to satellites, knows this new kind of mobility is cross-cultural. Very quickly everybody and their great-grandbabies were aboard. As time went on, I began to regret having made the phenomenon (i.e., cell phone disgust) central to the repulsory process that drove this novel, and not knowing how to deal with having written a book that was out of style before I had even finished it, forced me to put it away for a while.

Yet, in defense of that first draft, there was more to it than this antagonizing phone. There were place names: The Prado (a working class neighborhood), the Blue Match bar (this name subsequently removed), and B&H Dairy (the scene of at least two intertextual meetings, more on that later). There were relations: Monty the cab driver, the narrator's friend Largalos, Charlotte and Tom, and, of course, Frog. Nor must I forget Fred. There also was the film *Carla and Aïda*. The novella *After That* was going to stun you with its complexity. It would be big. "Big and long," I actually said to myself when I reached page sixty, having typed the new pages into the computer, very close to abandoning my notebook. It was probably very late fall 1998 when I said that.

One can say "big and long" and be talking about a small book. Does everyone know this? I do not think so. No, I do not think it has reached the public that small books are just as compelling as fat ones. Reader, it is all right for you to pull that slender volume away from the shelf and take it home; it is truly fine to place a slender volume of prose in the "fiction" section without worrying about it. It is. I have done it myself.

I finished the final version of the novella *After That* sometime late summer 2003, after two extensive re-writings and probably two (less intense) re-workings and countless line and paragraph edits, plus two shelvings and one almost utter shredding, and then I ran outside. The relief I felt was tremendous (though, ultimately, short-lived). "You have finished your novella," I told myself. "You have made a place for it." I was in my new city when I said this.

I had changed cities because I could not stand to see the demise of my old one, though I was aware that I had been living in its entrails for some time. But I do not think I need to reiterate my reasons for blinding myself to that reality. As it goes, I moved—many places at first, then finally settled on this one. "Why am I here?" I asked myself, walking among its thousands of ghosts. I could not find an answer but, in the interim, I met a girl and became enamored with her. She will be referred to as M.

I showed the novella to M.—once she had read my other work—and upon finishing it, she said "hmmm," studying me. We were in a very large park. I think she turned her head to see if this park mirrored the one referred to in the novel. "I didn't write it here," I explained to her. She did not appear to believe me. Well, people will think what they want. It is their right, I suppose. But *After That* could never have been written in this city.

I wrote it in a place of perpetual sun, a place that never rose above thirty degrees Celsius (I've given up Fahrenheit in protest of the government) and never sank below ten, a place of crowds that did not overwhelm one, as they do here, a place whose incomparable ease explains the near flatness of the writing, this flatness, which I could never alter and always haunted me.

That first summer in my new city, the sensation of my own flatness was very strong. With M. in the park, I was struck by the persistence of it. This feeling, which I thought I had rid myself of (by simply maturing as a person) had never left me. It had just taken on another form, manifesting itself differently, yet deeper, with every subsequent book. It strikes often at the end of a day, when I am reviewing some work I have just written, and I find myself thinking that it is not writing that I have done. It is speech, or air, plain air. It is zero. It is a gesture, a sign, an indication of writing. But, not writing, not at all writing.

On November 17, 1999, I recorded the following in my journal:

> [JH] wrote me, in response to AT, about one's losing sight of one's work as soon as one has begun it (as though I'm viewing a film of my writing projected on a screen behind me but it is I who have moved my chair so as to be obscured from it). Yes— that angle of looking almost up and back is what I'm thinking, which one's self orchestrates. So—will I ever see this book?

Five years later I have to answer "No." Not only will you not see that book but when you return to that note some years hence, older and in a new century, you won't even understand what you meant.

How many journals did I fill with questions of how to grasp this novella? Why after the many times I printed and held it in my hands, and even turned it toward others, did it never feel finished? Writing is a two-pronged process: there is ink-on-paper and there is absorption. I had attained the first quite easily, but was never satisfied with the second. Odd since it was only me—what I had seen, heard, invented—that I poured into this work, the same self I am using in this eulogy. It should have been easy. But absorption—the utter comprehension that a thing has been written to completion—I never fully achieved. Can you even speak of something that has refused to metabolize? In the final days of each of the drafts I wrote of the novella *After That*, I thought not.

The day on which I sat and wrote those first six pages fell a few weeks after I had read Marguerite Duras' *The Slut of the Normandy Coast* and a week or so after viewing Peter Greenaway's *The Falls*. It is amazing the things we think have affected us, especially in retrospect. But I encountered those things and started that book quite fluidly, so there must have been some correspondence there. In the concrete city where I wrote the first two drafts of the book, I had access to film in a way I never had before. You could go to theatres that were only a few blocks from where you lived and sit down in Italy or England or Taiwan, but you did not have to scramble for your Rough Guide usage books because the words the actors spoke were transferred to you, in your language. It was a technology people said little about, which had a terrific impact on my nightlife. I could be away without the distance being so far that I became self-conscious. In the end, I would see two or three films during my time in that city that I would return to repeatedly.

I realize that I have said little about the film that acted on the propulsion side of the unfolding of AT, a description of which inspired someone I highly respected to inquire as to its availability. You cannot imagine the pleasure I derived from that experience, and how much it was furthered by my answering, "It's a festival film, hard to find, impossible to rent." People did not "Google"; I knew my lie was safe. And that is what I am saying about lying: it can give one a much better high than can fiction. Plus, what does it mean to write fiction? What does fiction refer to?

The film *Carla and Aïda* was directed by the up-and-coming Anna Bailey. It was a hit with the art crowd and, more significantly, *we* loved it. Not only because it was shot in the city where we lived, but also because it patterned our lives perfectly. By "we" I mean me and the three other black lesbian artists I knew at this time. That's right, Carla and Aïda, the protagonists of Bailey's film, were lovers, not to mention painters, city travelers, and, to top it off, black girls. Who could believe it? Furthermore, they loved jazz and shared a home—albeit, one haunted by elusive narrating ghosts. Bailey had flipped some switch in us; people clamored to see her film.

But because everybody wanted to see it, my devoutly "alienated-and-proud" narrator refused to follow the pack, putting off her viewing until the last possible day, a day, unfortunately for her, full of conflict. This device of the "trek" or passage was a simple remedy to my earlier impasse with novel writing. As much as I had abhorred the idea of sequence as a poet, I realized that to tell lies or, at the very least, to write fiction one had to have several points from which to depart and at least one point at which to arrive. I would place my narrator in the early part of the morning and spend the novella getting her to the late evening. It is a simple device that then felt miraculous. Now I was novel-writing.

I am trying to remember when I finished that first draft, trying to picture when Frog might have lain in the sunlight splayed across her bed to masturbate. I am trying to picture this without being too inappropriate, as Frog (I mean Chubby) and I no longer share those feelings. I should be able to consult my journal, but for reasons unknown, I did not keep one at this time. But why is it so hard to go back in my mind and just see? I will have to write about the storage units that I rent on both sides of the United States to give a greater view of my disorientation. In the meantime, if I cannot simply turn to my mind to grasp the information that I need, then how else will I resolve this dilemma? The whole thing is very mysterious, a temptation to digress, and one I will resist.

In saying that I have two units on both coasts of the United States, I am saying that my withdrawal from my former city is not complete. I must figure out how to talk as someone occupying two places at once. But I shop in this new city; I eat here; currently, I write here. Tomorrow I am to recite my work before an audience, so also I read here. I do little in the former place that does not concern storage. So the simultancity is more abstract.

Excuse me.

—I am sorry and amazed that it has taken me so many pages (and years) to set this in concrete. To my defense, I have never been good at math. Plus, the idea that a late fall 1998 becomes an early winter 1999 instead of an early winter 1998 is mind-boggling. I believe the year should change at the end of summer, and never mid-season. Yes, I have been staring at the numbers all this time, and only today, this moment, did the puzzle solve itself. The novella *After That* was, without one remaining doubt, begun in the summer of 1998. In fact, it was idrotic (as we say in the South) to even consider that its inception could have occurred during the summer of 1999, when I have a journal entry that clearly states that I read from it in March of that year.

You will want to know why I don't just go back to the beginning of this work, erase the query over birth dates, and pretend that I've always known. Mainly, it is for the wash of relief I am bathing in right now that I want to press on. I think the relief more attractive than the perfection.

Also, many questions remain, and something else. I do not know if you have noticed, but there is no actual novella *After That* to accompany this report. The novella is not in the world. It is on the table, in a manila folder. It is not mine. That is, I do not have it in that important way one wants to have one's work. Nor do you have it.

There have been three distinct drafts of the novella; I have thus far told you about the first.

It was during the writing of the second draft of *After That* that I stopped referring to it as "AT," and began, somewhat curiously, to call it "AF." I have yet to find a note in my journal that comments on the change.

The majority of the second draft was written in a flat in a city connected to my former one by a bridge, such that it was, in effect, the same city. That is, I continued to work in the former city, commuting by train from my new home, and I continued to socialize there. No, it wasn't so much that these two places were the same city as it was that they had become an "area." Other people, sharing my predicament, thought in this way as well. Word had spread, and even those who lived exclusively in one or the other, thought themselves in "the area" too. "It does not matter how you live," I sometimes want to apply to the situation. It sometimes does not matter what you do in actual space. You just go on writing. I find that we exist in language and we exist on the city street, and that it is possible to believe you are doing one without knowing you are doing the other.

When I say, "we exist," I mean to be making a statement about urban living, how it goes on without one's full participation, how it insinuates itself in one's sentences. While I had been long aware that I was city living, I had not yet grasped that I was city writing too.

The second draft of the novella *After That* took shape while I lived on Filbert Street with my then lover S. Something had occurred between Frog and me that altered the intimacy between us; we remained friends, but on these opposing sides of the bridge. The situation did not last long, nor did it recover itself. Instead of moving back, I moved out, way out and over yonder, to the east coast of the country. From this I learned that it is possible to write a book based on your life in one place and continue it in another, and further possible to go on to live in several other places accomplishing the same goal. At least, this is true for a book that was written but never placed in the world.

Writing happened at a different pace on Filbert than it had on my previous streets. I was now writing in a house with mauve-colored walls; I was writing next door to a former crackhouse, which had become a lesser crackhouse and a place of violence. However, were you to read AF, in any draft, you would never encounter signs of the screaming or bloody shards of glass I witnessed there. That is one of the things fiction does for you.

The Filbert house was also the place where I began my "second" book, the one about the radicals. It was a spacious home, in which much reading and writing occurred, but not much sleeping. How can you sleep next to a threat of violence? How can you keep yourself from jumping out of your first floor window, running across the yard and yelling up to the fifth floor offender, "Get the fuck off her," when the scene has already been scripted for you, when you have already done it several times?

This same place was the house in which I turned thirty. It was the house where I became acquainted with the meat-alternative, tofu. It was the house where I donned a hat and stood in front of the refrigerator for a picture that would represent me to others. It was not a very good smile I gave, but I did not know this until later. I would not say I was at an advantage, and yet, time did pass. Months even, and somewhere along the way, I wrote the second draft of that novella, and somewhere else, a city off the radar beckoned me. Everything changed; we threw a party.

The gathering that took place in the backyard of the house on Filbert Street provided an opportunity for all the writers from both sides of the bridge to come together. We were in a good mood, though we did not obtain to orgy. We had barbecue and talked loudly to the various pets. An important photograph was taken. It was a time of leaving, and yet, the novella *After That* was not on my mind. I had finished the second draft some time before, perhaps to my satisfaction, and left it to appreciate. The moratorium was long.

But what have I said about the second draft other than it had been written? I also have told you where. You will want to know that I do not always remember writing this book, that when I turn my mind to it, these many years since its inception, I often do not recognize where I am. It is serious: I am sitting somewhere—a desk, a park bench—and suddenly a memory of the book is recalled to me. It gives me a feeling I wish to propagate, so I go inside for more. But it turns out that this thing we do by instinct, calling up a piece of our past to, in a sense, parade it before ourselves or others, can be awkward if that piece never fully existed in the world. I have said this before, but try holding it at the same time you are holding it. And that is how the mind fails. I call for it. "After That, come here," as if it were my animal. And most often something does come, usually a picture-feeling—a street combined with regret or longing—but once in a while, I call out and fog covers my thinking. Is this familiar? "After That?" I say, and observe the nothing and everything that overtakes me. A few tough moments elapse then, finally, a memory: yes, the house with mauve-colored walls and the desk that sat solidly in the warm room. Crossing "the area" on elevated transport also comes to mind, a navy blue Corolla, a neighbor named Lomarlo. But the writing, that immersion, the details of it elude me. This is due in part to tragedy. The things I lost while in that house, like the series of letters the bi-lingual poet had written me. These letters, for the writing of the second draft, were the only proof that I was getting something done, that a book was being made and re-made. Today, I call out to them, and all I get back is the image of a stack of light green pages, black ink, and the "trying" of left-handed script. On the bright side, however, and simultaneous to this immense feeling of loss, I have this realization: you can say anything about things that are not present. This is amazing. It is not quite like fiction, nor lying for that matter. It is something else. I am not daydreaming. It is more selfish than that.

One thing I grasped from all the film I watched during my stay in that concrete city, the city in which I wrote one draft of a novella that was later supplanted by a second draft, was that sequence and beauty could be arranged to devastating effect. While you can feel this way about many films, usually there will be one for which the sentiment is incontrovertible, a film that follows you in and out of cities, and in and out of books. That one for me is *Red Desert*, directed by Michaelangelo Antonioni.

My attachment to this film might have everything to do with this one line, a subtitle no less, that stayed with me as I exited the cinema—this was 1997; I was in my former city.

We are nearing the end of the film. What we have witnessed for the previous two hours is Monica Vitti careening along the edge of psychological disintegration, which Antonioni mirrors magnificently through a desolate, post-industrial landscape. At this point (where the line occurs), Vitti is in a critical state. She has just run from the apartment of a stranger with whom she was on the verge of having sex, though she is married with a young child; she stops in front of a motionless (red) train car (am I making this up?), it may even be raining. Vitti looks into the camera and gives a fairly long monologue about her struggles— how they have catapulted her from one disastrous event to another—that ends on this very exquisite, no doubt awkwardly translated note:

Everything I have done is my life.

Saying it to myself as I walked away from the theater, a tremendous pulse (I don't know how else to call it) thumped about inside me. I felt the original pulse and then a series of aftershocks. It was a quickening. Something wanting to happen.

It would be irresponsible for me not to admit that I am now uncertain that it was, in fact, 1997 when I saw this film, because the image of the street (myself walking down it) that goes along with the sensation of "Red Desert," is not appropriate to the apartment I occupied in 1997. It is true that I had many homes in the seven years I resided in that city, however, unlike the drafts of the novella *After That*, I remember precisely where and to what extent I occupied them. Why was I walking down Dubire, toward the Lower Eighth, when I lived on Capp Street, which lay in the opposite direction? The discrepancy complicates my ability to connect the awakening effect of having heard that line to everything I believed to have happened subsequently. But, I must go on with this story.

On January 28, 2000, I attended a reading at a popular local venue for experimentation. (I am still combing my journals for corroboration: I did write this book; I did try hard to write it.) I do not know whose reading it was, but in those days, I was in the habit of taking notes. This event was held in the city, where "the problem of the person"—my problem —was made evident. The notes I took kept the problem within reach, though the notes themselves were not always cogent. The reading must have really struck me, because from it I culled these words:

a text where the everyday means risking syntax

The person who wrote the first two drafts of the novella *After That* knew that there was something radical about walking down the street. She knew that the corners she turned, the people she came upon, the simplicity of their dialogue, had a tremendous impact on the flow of language. There was a way these events of living could not hold up against progress. Yes, one did go "there" after leaving "here," but instead of taking fifteen minutes (it's just five blocks away) it took three hours. You risked the syntax when you wanted to make a place for the gaps. In writing this novella, I needed to say, "I left the house," plainly, in orchestration with other plain sentences, such that their combining would produce a newer, deeper effect. All plain would somehow become all cloudy.

Two days after I had scribbled that line about risking syntax, I returned to my journal; something had occurred in my life or my thinking that recalled Antonioni to me. On January 30, I wrote:

> The thing I want with After That is Antonioni, not Fellini. Space and Void. Not clutter. Not chaos.

My challenge was to build, out of a series of empty spaces, a cohesive narrative long enough to be called a novella, but not so long nor so cohesive that it suffered from chronology, a thought that led me to this somewhat unfinished query:

> Does the unfolding of the narrator's world (i.e. her friends and history, her plans) produce the events?

Or what? I wonder. The novella *After That* was all about event, if I knew anything it was that. So there must have been something else, something more slippery I wanted to say. I am surprised that I did not try harder to work this problem out. Did I mean: can an event occur through the simple introduction of a name or relation, or must the event be planned outside the boundary of the text and then dropped in? A distinction I wonder at today. I mean, what *does* produce events in writing? It seems that the words of this language are greatly inclined to associate. They seek each other out; they make a group. This groups seeks out the next group, soon they are a community, a city. You only need a word to write a novel. You only need half a word to write a novella. I had that half word; it was *ong–*. It did its part. Events were produced and strung along. There were 18,745 words, twenty-two events, twenty one intervals, seven characters, five place names, a film, a fight, and an underground adventure. Had my half-word been *lug–* would things have configured differently? In any case, I ended that entry with these words:

Sequence, Aesthetics, Deliverance.

"Aesthetics," I never found out what that meant, and "Deliverance" is a movie I have never seen. But "Sequence" I thought I should know enough about. I did not return to writing about AF until February 9:

How to achieve Antonioni, which is grace.

I was still after him.

And finally, this list:

(In my journal, the word "grace" is written in the top right corner, not exactly flush)

1. The simplicity of scenes—so themselves that there is no need to add or force. A kind of honesty (if only the character believes it, effuses it) that's pervasive.

2. Language as delicacy, as abstracted beauty, as brushed or drawn onto the page, that reveals, strives, up-ends itself.
3. Awareness of meta-presences: silence, absence, light or dark of day, grays of meaning, peripheral reality, sound or gestures of living.
4. Arrival and then displacement. Impermanent realization; tender leaving of clarity.

I must admit a lack of conclusiveness that I wrote the above statements. It is one of those things. There are no signs of having quoted another source, but there is something other about this list. If it is yours I apologize. How did I get it? In any case, what a recipe for success! If you follow these steps, don't you end up writing the novel of the century? How can you not?

Again, I must interrupt the flow of this report to discuss a problem. I have been thinking. Where does the first draft of a work end and the second draft begin? And if that separation is assessable, which would seem only fair, is it possible to continue this distinguishing into further drafts? Sometimes, it is the case that changes to a text are not extreme enough to transform that current version into a newer one. So, does one actually count these minor fixings as draft-making? These questions stand in for the three months that have passed since I contributed anything to this report. It has been another archival dilemma. Instead of worrying over the drafts themselves, perhaps I should focus my attention on the gaps between these intensive periods of writing; it is probably these moments that could explain what is ultimately a failure to actually produce said novella. However, while I find the fact of this failure huge and interesting, I should not let it distract me from my greater intention. The unfurling of the book.

I began the novella *After That* in July of 1998. I wrote prolifically for eight or nine months. I even "finished" it. Chubby and I were still lovers. She was the first to read that draft and was kind enough to come as a response to it. The second draft was written between late fall of 2000 and early spring 2001, while I was a resident of the city adjacent to my former one. The interval of late spring 1999 to early fall 2000 is not like the interval of late spring 2001 to late spring 2003. In the former, I was celebrating what I believed to be the end of this particular era of writing (having finally trumped my previous eight-page novel attempts), while in the latter I seemed to have removed AF from my mind entirely, as if I had decided that it would be one of two endeavors in my life that I did not complete. (Many years later, it became the one.) I had given up on it, presumably for newer complexes of sentences.

However, out of some string of events, having to do with aging and groundlessness, I made my way back to AF in the summer of 2003. I wanted to apply the future (what I had learned) to the past (my then limits), in that way we have long been discouraged from doing. The books I had written in the interim were accomplished in their novelistic approaches (I had finished them), so why not go back and fix this one? Could I plant these innovations without destroying the structure of my 1998 thinking? I did not want to make a new book; I wanted to salvage this old one. I wrote on that third (and final) draft through late fall, and finished it in spring 2004.

Something subtler than the distinction between drafts has crept in. Suddenly I feel the need to make a differentiation between a draft (which one is presently writing) and the other task to which I've been referring— "finishing." The impulse for these two activities would have to be different; in one you surrender, in the other you progress. At least, you hope to surrender, you hope to progress. I think I did both of these things. I did not write about them explicitly, and I did not categorize the work this way, but I can recall both behaviors and can associate them with the novella *After That*. But can I say when I did one rather than the other? Is not every draft an attempt to finish? No, I do not think so. Sometimes you know there is a lot more to do.

What happened over the ten years it took Ralph Ellison to write *Invisible Man* and the fifteen (more or less) years it took Denis Diderot to write *Jacques The Fatalist?* Furthermore what happens between the silences of an author's successive novels? And those of us who write several books simultaneously, what keeps the whole thing from bleeding?

In my new city, the one that grows solidly gray during the hot summer, I have been thinking about cycles. The idea that my life is a collection of emotions cycling has made me somewhat depressed. That the sadness I feel for a particular thing over a particular time will be replaced or washed out by some good news that carries me for a while, which subsequently is dulled by a period of confusion—that confusion becoming complexity resulting in the writing of a book, whose subsequent deliverance in the world creates happiness, then numbness. To see all of this repeating, when I am so hot and live so far away from the center of my new city, is more than I can bear. But even that is somewhere in the cycle.

The novella *After That* is one of the few cycles in my life to come to a flat, unalterable end. There is nothing, beside this report, to represent it. In fact, as far as the general public is concerned it never existed. Even the books that do exist, often seem to not really. Well, this despondent feeling—that one is alone in the world and the things one creates matter to about four people—is not a new despondency: I became a person in its midst. But, now, I want to grow old thinking something different, like, public space *does* exist, or publicity *is* my friend.

Many pages ago I wrote, "There is fiction and then again there is life." As long as I was writing first person narratives, I was always in life, even if it was an embellished one. However, the moment I began to write about Carla and Aïda, as occurrences beyond the reach of my narrator, giving them their own "parts" in the book, I began to write another kind of narrative. I want to ask Nathalie Sarraute about the voice that talks back to her in her novels, but she is deceased now. I want to know if the presence of that other ever made her question whether it was fiction she was writing. I want to ask my dog Eva to come here, to try a piece of this pear I am eating, but she is deceased as well. Am I in fiction?

I have found proof in my journals that in mid-March 2000 I was obsessed with identifying the tone of my sentences with that of other writers. There were things about reading I did not understand, like the connection between my eyes and your page. I wondered how it was possible to immerse myself in the reading of a certain work, to feel in that work that I was staring into a mirror, and yet when it came time to produce my own writing, to have that sound be so radically different. It was Henry James whose work I had thought I breached. Having absorbed nearly everything he wrote, it seemed natural that the lushness of his prose would become my lushness. I wrote as a Jamesian, with a jacket and a cane, and tried to turn my characters into labyrinths. It was easy to move my hands across the keyboard as though my language was flowing, but it proved difficult to turn my eleven word sentences into his eighty.

Inevitably, one kind of reading leads to another kind, and it was this moving from author to author that allowed me to cover ground as to the nature of my tone.

While visiting a writer in a faraway place, I came upon a book written by the then unknown to me French writer Hervé Guibert; it was a novel written after the author had contracted HIV and was moving into the onset of AIDS. This book—the first of a series of his that I would come to read—was called (in translation) *To the Friend Who Did Not Save My Life*. All the time I was reading, I was confounded by the fact that Guibert's narration— the precise tone of the language—was just barely stylistic. It was almost reportage. Almost. Because at the same time that this flatness existed (flatness meaning an ease or directness of storytelling, also a feeling of being held to the surface) there also was present another quality that I could not name. I soon found this same undefined flatness in Julio Cortázar's prose. By "undefined" I mean that this sound, which created in me a question of whether I was actually reading at all, should have been drawn out and studied, but as far as I could tell it had not been. On April 28, 2000, I recorded the following:

> The book that approximates the simplistic character of my work is *The Gangsters* by Hervé Guibert. There are differences of course. He appears less conscious of the permeability of the moment [that the act of writing can take on a character role] which is my present occupation, but there is something in the narrative tone that we share. His work bears a suspicious ease in storytelling—suspicious because something in it makes it unapparent. It's like the language glides though somehow it shouldn't, but I can't say why. Whatever the reason, it must be related to what peculiarizes my work. But can't see it yet.

Two and a half months later I ended another entry on this note:

> My work is easy. It seems to say, "Walk along here happily." But what I'm attempting to do is make the reader suspect this progression, suspect whether she is in fact progressing. It's amazing how much you can do with tone. How with confidence the narrator can say, "I am walking on my head," and though the reader knows this is impossible, there is still the declaration of the narrator to deal with. You have to both progress and stall when you have a paragraph made of such sentences. That's what I want: to move and go nowhere.

Though I was struggling "to move and go nowhere" in my work, in that concrete city, I began more and more to live the experience—walking up and down the same streets, avoiding the same boutique people. The city had changed dramatically from 1999 to 2000, but in such a negative way that it did not provide the necessary spark. Yet, all that time I was thinking about sentences, and trying to get them to tell me about terrain, the grid in particular. But it is only now that I can say this. Then, it was more that I was thinking of language on the one hand and thinking of city on the other, not putting the two together, except literally. Walking and thinking. So it was important that I stayed to these streets, that I continued to wander them though I knew absolutely where I was going. I was enamored with the flatness of the grid, the streets repeating themselves, their names as numbers ascending or descending, their names as places pointing self-referentially; the grid was comforting in its repeating and in the message that it gave: this is city, you are in a city, keep walking.

The place on the other side of the bridge that combined with my former city to make an "area" was also immensely flat. My next city was flat and so was the one following it. That story is in these sentences.

But how late it has become. I should have turned around pages ago. And I would have were it not for the novella *After That,* which is not quite buried. In this kind of writing, it is hard to know how much you want to say about a thing that you are calling a failure. You are here because of it; it makes you want to bring in your life. It also makes you say its name repeatedly. However, at some point, the story itself must come out, that is, the precise details of the novella we have been talking about—what happened and to whom. Dear reader, what follows is the authorized version:

Our narrator, whom we will refer to as R for the purpose of this exegesis, awakes on the last day on which to see a film directed by Anna Bailey, which is starred in a touring film festival. The film *Carla and Aïda* is a hit in some circles and has received the great prize from Berlin.

On this morning (which begins with a wake-up call from her lover Frog) R is preparing to leave the house to accomplish a list of errands before her eight o'clock film when her neighbor Charlotte drops in to borrow a half-cup of sugar. Charlotte appears agitated. She is speaking on a cell phone. After escorting Charlotte to the kitchen and pointing out the sugar jar, R excuses herself to shower. When R returns she is surprised to find that Charlotte is still there, now yelling into her phone at a "Tom" and stirring waffle batter. Charlotte seems unmoved by R's re-appearance. R decides to consider the situation from a comfortable chair in the living room. After running through the events four or five times, studying the irregularities, R realizes that the house has been silent for several minutes. She goes to check on Charlotte; the new scene is just as startling. Charlotte has gone, and not only did she leave behind her cell phone, for reasons R cannot begin to imagine, but also she, most egregiously, absconded with R's waffle iron.

Following some peaceful then aggressive attempts to get back her waffle iron, R takes a short nap. When she wakes, she gathers her things and heads out to run a day of errands. At the bottom of her bag is Charlotte's cell phone, which she is hoping to exchange for her iron somewhere along the way.

She walks through her favorite part of the city.

She enters another part of the city. She passes the bookstore, outside of which are hanging a group of people she calls "the true underground," or sometimes just "the trues." These are people who have held indignantly to their ideals, who have not been lost to consumerism or an over-invested public identity. They are beyond categories of cool. R struggles to be "true" today with this new possession; she worries that at any moment it will ring, which would be humiliating. She walks quickly passed the group. Fortuitously, it is a block later that the phone rings. She answers to shut it up. It is that "Tom" from before. They have an uncomfortable conversation. He is yelling at her.

He wants something, and believes she is Charlotte. He is also in pain; someone on his side is beating him up. They get disconnected, though not before Tom tells her to "bring the stuff."

[To interject, I added this criminal element—the above insinuation of some "dark" doings by Charlotte and Tom—in the final draft. After years of asking, "What's missing?" it occurred to me that I needed to beef up the mystery. In previous drafts, the phone just rang and rang, but she never answered it. This was when I believed the sheer presence of the cell phone would be plot enough to explain her aversion to it, before everyone I knew owned one.]

R continues her walk. She passes a bar in which some white hipsters are mistreating a drunken man that R identifies as Mexican. The man wants to enter the bar; the hipsters, who are bartending, do not want him. R intervenes. She and the main hipster have an altercation, not physical but violent nonetheless, which ends with a blast from the cell phone and R's retreat around a corner.

R hails a taxi. One stops. The driver is her acquaintance Monty. She is happy to see him, but cannot climb aboard: his advertising is appalling. R waves Monty on. The gesture is both mad and guilty. Her situation worsens: the phone rings again. She pulls it out, yells at it, throws it to the ground, picks it up, then sprints for an approaching bus.

On the bus, once she calms down, once she settles into its air-conditioned lull, she begins to fantasize about Carla and Aïda—not as characters of Bailey's film but as real people she is bound to encounter. She projects them onto the city, moving along the streets, sitting in cafés, lounging in the park, until the smell of pastries disrupts her daydreams. The person next to her is eating doughnuts. R gets up from her seat and moves toward the back of the bus.

The first part of the novella *After That* ends there; I titled it "Corridor," which leads to "Landing," part two. Here, we are not in the time of R but in that of her projections, what might happen were one to will one's daydreams to fruition. It begins:

Ascertaining the difficulty of a life that approximates your own, when you wake up next to it, touch it, and feed it, when you call that life Aïda, and your name is Carla. You do not feed on that life —you share your utensils with it. You watch it dress, study its body, note the changes in it. If your name is Carla, memory carries you through life. You have not written anything. You have a lack of trust in the world. You love and suspect your growing public. Your name is Carla as much as your life is art, is Aïda.

***

Then there is the first morning you wake after having been on stage, the pain in your back from childhood that wakes you, the last vestige of dream material drawn from your night on the screen. Aïda does not look like you, except for her arms. And it's not that you are calmer or that her temper bothers you. And though her art is younger, her ideas swarm around you. Every morning you fight off what's leaked over from her dreams.

When she wakes you won't tell her. You'll let her go on thinking.

She does not recognize anything about the screen.

It's not your job to show it to her. You retreat into your painting room, place earthen colors on the spotted wood table, and begin.

I used the next ten pages to explore the idea of seepage—not only that phenomenon of thought where the thing under scrutiny gets pressed into the folds of reality [this to explain the occasions when R glimpses Carla or Aïda moving through the city] but also how that pressed thing creates its own folds in which a newer unreal is caught up [this to explain Carla and Aïda's sightings of R]. In this part, we spend time in each of the painter's studios and are exposed to the impact of music on their work. We hear about Glenn Spearman and Alice Coltrane.

In "Stairs," part three, we return to the principal narrative, to R staring from the window of the bus, contemplating trees and passing storefronts. It is one of those situations where you are not quite present in yourself and all of a sudden something familiar catches your eye and calls you back. R spots Charlotte turning a corner. She leaps from the bus and runs after the fleeing figure, to no avail. The exertion exhausts her. R lies down in the street to rest. The day is too hot.

After some complications regarding the t-shirt she is wearing (it is too tight), her missing bottle of water, and the nagging cell phone, she manages to get up. It is midday. She fusses with her appearance for several blocks in anticipation of her meeting with Fred. When she reaches him, he welcomes her. Their interaction runs smoothly until he discovers that she is in possession of a cell phone. His response is severe. He pushes her down a manhole. A moment later, he throws himself down. Once they recover, they take a long walk underground; he delivers several speeches. They stop someplace and watch water dripping from a pipe, which makes them sleepy. They nap. R has a dream.

In the dream she follows Carla (or is it Aïda?) around the city. A group of watchers observe her. There is some ambiguity as to whether she is dreaming them or they her. The boundary between them blurs. [At first, I'm surprised by this turn in the narrative, then I begin to see what it does, complicating the event structure. But, to take advantage of what I've done, I've got to find the meta-feeling and get it across to the reading. I bury myself in making the watchers a becoming-narrative itself. Thinking it is like a dream. I wake up, then she wakes up.]

R opens her eyes. She does not know how long she has been sleeping, but Fred is gone and her body is intact. It is time to get going. She makes her way to ground level and walks a while trying to find her bearings. In Chinatown, Charlotte's phone rings. R answers and has a disturbing conversation. Tom again, threatening. He wants what he wants. But Charlotte has it, not she.

Evening approaches as R makes her way to Frog, the reclusive lover for whom she has agreed to shop and run errands. She strikes through the list of tasks without mishap, then returns to Frog for supper. All is calm, until sudden ringing forces her to disclose the cell phone. Then there is only frenzy. Frog has never seen one. She must get closer. She wants desperately to hold it. Her restraint is buckling. She grabs it; she hands it back; she grabs it again, and then turns away decisively. She runs, locks herself in the bathroom.

R leaves her to it. She considers the day done, except for her movie. But there is time to sit here before it starts. She goes to the cushy chair near the window and climbs in, giving way to exhaustion. Exhaustion—that events press upon one, despite all categorical resistance, despite R's unwillingness to rise and complete what she started. She stays there, with her gaze turned inward. The narrative departs, moves down the street, culls without her.

R lets us go. There is little else to do but close part four, known by the title "Lobby." From this place, we go to the realm of the indefinite—the projections' projection—in part five, called "View." I hold you here while I try to say something about fiction, while for the first time I allow myself to think about "fiction." Here it is, in its entirety, below:

27

In a week, there has been little progression on the painting, except for our discreet touches. Aïda, preoccupied with the corner of her room that we know least about, has developed a strange habit of looking over her shoulder once every five or ten minutes in a gesture of alarm. We are worried that she has become aware of us. But could this be true? That's our guilt. We have lost confidence that our observations are wholly aesthetic in nature, not conspiratorial or predatory, and so to be safe are staying over here near the unfinished painting.

The house has been quiet all week—both women trying to get work done. Sounds have been reduced to early Chico Hamilton, Guillermo Portabales, and, of course, Alice Coltrane. The painters meet occasionally in the hall, reserved and ghostly. Aïda talks about Zora Neale Hurston; Carla offers encouragement. On occasion, one will stand in the doorway of the other's painting room, in silence, not looking at the work but the painter working, possibly asking, "Do I look like this?" Standing there, the one will travel a bit—from the arms that will remind her of walking to the neck and shoulders shining with sweat or shadow, then eventually off the body and along a plane in nearby space, seeing images or hearing soft music—until the other realizes that the one is standing there, who then waves and walks on.

***

In the kitchen there are two slices of bread in the toaster that popped up fourteen hours ago, in the hall some boxes that Aïda dragged in. Despite the subtlety of events, there is a heightened level of excitement. Finishing, not unlike preparing for death, has stylized this household. Even our barely solid forms glow with some odd polish.

(Since the day we entered we have struggled to gain footing here. It's not that we have opponents. It's the task itself—rendering the lives of others—that is troubling and incomplete. How ironic! They are finishing, but it is we who are making confessions. Giving testimony, as though we were the specimens—)

Sometimes, and we hesitate in revealing this, Carla grabs Aïda from behind and devours her. We are trying to present the event as art, which is the only reason it has been recorded. The last time, Aïda was in the middle of drawing a horizontal line across the top quarter of the canvas (which she subsequently replaced with a continental shape in the color green). Carla's sudden passion and its contagion after she grabbed Aïda startled us into rapt attention. The art we are trying to qualify is in timing—noting the perfect intervals. Carla's clenched thighs moving at various tempos between Aïda's legs is a distinct interval to be explored.

(Well, having said that, we cannot agree on whether it's appropriate to reproduce this scene. A debate ensues: Is this our work? Is it art? What ought the reader know? Until we tire ourselves. However, one point on which we are in accord is the futility of omnipresence.)

To repeat, for many days, the house has been ensconced in the silence of finishing. All but the essentials have been shut out. We remain because we are a gift to the environment. That's the first lesson in being trained: recognize your role as conveyor. Without us, there would be no events. Yes, there would be two painters in their respective rooms trying to finish their work, but no one would have access to them. It would be as though they only existed for the phantom pleasure of the isolated event. Our gift is that we are interested enough to create a string, whereby they and others can identify patterns in time, see people.

Between the two painters, there are three to five groups of hosts, who are not capable of knowing each other. We are separated by the camera, which hails and exiles us from our assigned realities. The camera has a limitation, though. It can only capture a certain circumference of space in a single shot, such that the occurrences lying outside its line of vision, the occurrences, which very well may be what gives shape to the "captured" space, are removed of any particularities. This shortness of field becomes popular reality, or an even more debated word, fiction.

***

When Aïda withdraws from the mystery she engages in the corner of her studio to return to us and the painting, there is discord between time (spent away) and event (of the painting's progress). Yet it is difficult to add these subtleties to the fiction. We have failed, so far in this narration, to explain that Aïda undergoes a change each time she walks away from the canvas and that this change influences the unfolding work. One can't see it exactly. The work is infused with the change—the image already completed. In a sense, she has performed all actions and undergone all growth and dispersion necessary to finish this last work of the series, yet the absence of the visual remains.

28

"This teeters along the thin line between the abstract and the supernatural," Carla thinks every time the fabric is lifted, though not in those words. "I'm confounded by sound," again not precise but close enough.

After a few moments, she grabs a sketchbook and settles into the sofa, almost says:

"It's hard to understand how to resolve in one medium that which occurs solely in another—the honk of a saxophone—without having to resort to the figurative or an abstraction that does not know itself. This has always been my question. How does one put what one hears in music into language or a visual form? Moreover, how does any translation happen? Even now as I think of what I want—the inscription of my thoughts onto paper in acrylic or whatever substance—versus what I have—some mess on a board—even as I attempt this honk in my own form, the honk itself has escaped me. I have to replay the song. I do, but before I can articulate the honk, it's gone."

She thinks, "I haven't moved."

What shows on the 32"X24" sheet of paper does not reflect any of what she's saying. The drawing is clearly musical. The intervals are placed with skill and obvious compass-clarity, and the honk of the horn blares—there, across the bottom, where the red and black lines meet vertically and concave at the same time. How is it that she does not see? And why are we always asking this question? The event—what one has made— always seems to lie behind or ahead of the person, which in a sense, because we are so bound to the present, puts us in an uncomfortable position: observing the reality that no one wants to enter. The reality in which that person is so intricately scripted.

The sofa faces the canvas, but the shadows creeping across the work make it difficult to assess from where she's sitting. So though she's looking at it, we know she doesn't see it. This is infuriating for some of us. (It is agreed that the observer has the ability to influence the chronology of things, but the reason that she doesn't is for fear of being brought into the scene, made to act.) The fury we feel at the neglect of the present works itself out in our projections. We create fiction.

She sits in front of the canvas with sketchbook in hand, gazing intensely at the painting, as though she were inside it. The book is open to a page, which to us appears covered in mathematical symbols. There is an "x", a "b," and perhaps an "a," then several short horizontal lines floating in between. But, perhaps what appears to be "a" is a face or a dactyl. We are hovering over her right shoulder, pushing each other around in order to assume all perspectives. Everyone directs the other to some place else. Soon we move to the left shoulder, then above her head and ultimately to the floor between her legs, recording furiously the intricacies of her actions. These actions that, if seen only from the front are non-existent, turn in on themselves from down here.

Someone has told me to take a break here. Someone called and said, "You should take a break. The reader will grow tired of the past." This is fine, as I need to stop and place a feeling that has come over me. I am writing a book about the failed writing of another book, and gingerly placing the events of that failing in a circuit of time; yet, days and years are passing in this memorial. It is the middle of the night; I am cold. I am wrapped in a blanket in neither my old nor my once-new city. Three books exist in my mind: the first draft that became the novella *After That,* the last draft that seemed to reach completion and erasure in the same instance, and this telling of those drafts (plus some minor ones). The books lay on top of one another, and next to them, if you lift that long sheet of parchment, you will find five others. Not related to this writing but not unrelated either. I am afraid to tell you where I am, what this place looks like. It does not follow the trajectory of the previous places I have lived. It is "easy" like the first one and "old" like the second, but it is up and away and cold and empty like nothing else I have endured. But beautiful, in that nothing has taken its light away. It does not fog; it does not suffocate. It glows. I try to glow with it. This is not always possible.

But, you have to finish what you started, so you use your insomnia.

When I realized that I was staring over the shoulder of an earlier staring over the shoulder, I asked my friend about it, and she recommended this surcease. Since page one, I have been writing myself into a book that already bore "me"; and now, nearing its end, I have multiplied myself again. I am writing about the writing about the writing of that long ago book. Hundreds of sheets of novella crowd this room. I am sleepless and cold and warm and walking through all the time that does not write the book. I am full of overlapping views. This looking over Carla's shoulder, I feel I have been standing here for most of my life. How amazing it is to think that everything from that world will vanish, that this book will finish the other one. The many desks and chairs will be thrown into the closet; the ghost of the book, still not free, will move on to the next emerging novel. I will have closed the book. I close it.

29

So finishing has caused dissent among the viewers, proving that it is not always easy to speak collectively. We are struggling to distinguish the occurrences that take place in the subject's mind from those events of the room, as the camera has a way of making it all available. That is the crux of our infighting and, subsequently, our excuse for any inconsistencies. However, in the meantime, we have agreed to pass on the "problem" of the camera.

Our example:

Two or three characters sit in a room having many unrelated thoughts; they all have hot drinks and brown arms and are looking at each other. If one counted the utterances from each of them and then all as a group, the sum would be five consecutive conversations. Music plays in the next room. Each conversation is related to the others by gestures and small words, all five spinning along some, as yet, undiscovered mishearings. The camera shows one character speaking against the profile or back of another, such that the frame is divided into various angles. When the level of interaction intensifies—for instance, there is a disagreement between them—the camera decides against using a volley to portray the scene. Instead, those viewing are fed a wide, unaltered shot. When the dynamics of the scene reach the point of near dispersion (as resulting from too much energy) the camera struggles to hold the room. This is a still, and yet the clutter and contrast of shelves, books, walls, framed paintings, and enflamed conversation pushes the scene to the edge. The camera jostles it and messes up the shot. A frame is lost.

To recover, the camera turns and rests on a vacant room, the first on the left when facing the hall. It's a painting room. There are a few easels and a large chalkboard, cast in evening shadow. The camera remains locked on the contents on the left-hand side of the room. Minutes go by.

There is nothing to narrate, exactly. But as hosts, we have to stand up.

We feel the camera's eye on us, though it would be more accurate to describe it as a finger that points a command to make the scene known. We stretch out of our crouched and dormant positions to collect variances. The camera retreats to the furthest corner, but is still in charge.

And when we are fully extended, that is, showing that we are clearly the hosts, we begin to narrate the scene. Since there are no people present in this room of our habitation, we describe the inanimate contents. We report the day each piece of furniture was dragged into the room; we reveal secrets behind the cracks in the wall (saying who threw what where). And the books, we pull them off shelves with pride, as though each author were a longtime companion. This is a performance, which continues until we are satisfied that there is a definite shape to the room, an image that will remain after we have crawled back to our former positions.

But sometimes there is the silence of waiting because we have not said enough. Time elapses and nothing happens to our picture of the room. The camera wants more, but we are happy with what we have given. In some cases, the impasse lasts for days.

But in this example, something in another part of the house calls the camera back. There is laughter emanating from the peopled room; the camera goes to it messily.

In trying to re-adjust to the lost frame, particulars have been missed. We "wake" when the camera returns, but are too far behind. We begin to compromise the story line. More people have shown up. We decide to use psychology to explain this: the painters were lonely and so invited friends over; once they invited these friends they became greedy and invited more. The friends have stayed for what seems like days. There are nine of them in the kitchen, standing and slapping their hands against their thighs. The camera is excited, trying to insist on relation, that we can read it.

However, translation is a difficult task when one enters the conversation after the fifth word, when all remaining words in the speech are dependent on that very first. We try to talk to the others; to ascertain what they have heard from their positions (in nearby rooms). But their words don't carry in the roar of the present, which overwhelms.

We realize that we haven't explained the camera at all (for instance, what it's doing here in fiction) and now we see that we've gotten away from the purpose of our current narration: the finishing of Carla and Aïda. In fact, there is a growing suspicion that we altogether went wrong. That is, what deeper notions of experience could we have conveyed had we said more about voice or the elasticity of character? What if we had given the details of events, rather than our impressions? Would you have a book in your hand, fiction?

Regardless, it appears that the lamentable hurdle that separates parts from their sum has been cleared. Fragments have coagulated into products to be weighed, and if lucky, admired. The remaining objective, we can describe only as punctuation. For Carla, the closing gesture is a deep red drawn to connect two intervals that appear flooded by the vacuity of untranslatable sound. While Aïda adds lines along the periphery, which she projects will create a better balance within the frame. The paradox of finishing a painting is that the final stroke or touch, as soon as it is completed, is immediately absorbed into the entirety of the work. The process by which one arrived at the end is not discernible to the viewer, the specifics are relegated to autobiography. When one finishes a work, whose culmination seemed unattainable, one is overwhelmed mostly by the fact that she made it. A stunned silence, different from the silence of concentration, descends.

(So that you know, there is a disagreement as to how this portrayal should end. A few believe that ending a work in a gesture of theory is a sign of abandonment, while others argue that the distance conditions the reader. One or two believe a narrative should complete itself by returning to the point of its origination. We cannot come to terms, but it hardly matters. Even if we could agree on an ending, our sense of events unfolding in time would never correspond to that of the painters. The reader still would be left with an undermining suspicion that something was off.)

Carla and Aïda are moving toward the end of an epoch in postures awaiting the cessation of time, unaware that time has already recounted its steps and begun again. When they arrive at the end, it looks like the end and they sit there in it, for days. They give in to the marvel of accomplishment; friends come over, drink and eat cake. They deride the hardships of the past, though not without some ongoing deference to it. They speak quietly about the new beginning, guess at its shape and progression.

On the sixth or seventh day of celebration, a sensation, awakening in the furthest, most forgotten region of their bodies, begins to creep to the popular side. One of them wakes with a start insisting to the other that she almost died in a dream or that she saw herself incredibly old. During the next few nights, other images follow—all involving changes to the body or the hovering of ideas whose full form elude them. The succession and obvious connection between dreams hold the two in a state of wonder. Time still moves at the microscopic level, now an eighth through each painter's next life, which she has not yet thought to enter.

The introduction of "the beginning" into their consciousness comes at the end of a subtle accumulation of events. It unnerves them like a flu or a fever in the middle of the night. One expresses the symptoms of its arrival, while the other gives the diagnosis: they have lost synonymy with time. The predicament is one that they have seen before, though they always forget. For once it shows itself, the unbearable pressure of its seclusion lifts.

So there it is. What went wrong? Is it obvious to the reader? Nicole Brossard wrote in the preface of her project *Journal Intime*, "[T]he journal seems to me a place where the subject turns around and around to the point of exhaustion." I had thought this was also the definition of fiction. Is it possible that I was mistaken? Did I exhaust myself thinking I was writing fiction when really I was just exhausting myself? Is the reader also exhausted, because how strange is it to read the final chapters of a book whose previous chapters remain (mostly) unknown to one? But alternately, how does one write the story of a novel—eulogize it—without incorporating it somehow?

Ironically, these last chapters did have a life in the world, if just a Canadian life, if just a periodic, experimental Canadian life, where they appeared under the title "Watchers" in a magazine called *Matrix*. You will only print your coda when you are desperate, as I had been, between the second and third drafts of this book. I had written nearly one hundred pages of a day in the life of four years in the living of me, if that is clear. And they were stalled, thus I was stalled. When a friend asked me to contribute work to a project she was guest editing, I thought, here is my chance to get this book moving again. The piece was accepted; the issue eventually came out. However, nothing much changed for the novella *After That*.

In March of 2004, I retrieved the book from the drawer for the last time. "Let me see it," I thought. "Now I'll know what to do." Time passed in which I had grown, and many things had happened to me, among them the writing of another novella-length book. It seemed fair to conclude that whatever allowed me to finish the second book would help me heal the first. I pulled it out and to my dismay I still did not know what to do. It persisted in being unpublishable. Was I even in reality when I assessed this? What did I see? What was the actual book I was reading? When it is just you, you cannot really answer those questions. But, yes, something was missing. The writing of the third (and final) draft occurred in a time where I had moved to my new city but had yet to secure a place of residence there. I had a typing machine that made it possible to do many things and be "nowhere" at the same time. I could stop and write between places as well as I could write from their centers. During this period, I was living in a village on the east side of a city. There were many cars and pizza shops and languages to rest in or feast upon, yet I was very lonely there. I pulled the novella *After That* out of the drawer because I believed it to be the root of my problem with prosperity. I had taken on the weight of an un-circulating work (only four people had read it in its entirety) and did not know how to get rid of it. I wrote the last draft of the book with the scope I had gained from my recent ventures in fiction but could not find peace with it. What was wrong? It was not mine anymore. Yet it was no one else's either. It had to go on with me. Had it belonged to another, perhaps it would have made its way into the world and I, though in a very different way, could have had it. But what I have been saying is that it was devastating—after completing then promptly rejecting that last draft—to have written a book and to have lost it and to be holding it there all at once. The novella *After That*, I finally had to say, would never be a book in the world. I sat in that disappointment for several minutes (I may even have gotten out of my chair and walked glumly around the apartment. I probably returned to my chair and sat more glumly then once again got up.) At some point, it occurred to me that though I could not have the book I could have the story of its failure and that perhaps this would be enough. I grabbed my notebook and wrote the opening with ease, as if this piece had run parallel all along. It read:

> "Let me see it," as strange as this sounds, was my first thought when I returned home this evening. Hours before—having printed the last page of the manuscript and prepared to flee the house—I'd written "After That: a novella" across the title page, then I ran outside. When I was about a block from home I turned around and came back. I pulled the manuscript out again—a crisp stack of ninety-seven very white, very smooth pages—and scribbled in black ink "When I was a poet" just under the title to qualify things. I changed my outfit, adding a new, more versatile layer (a hooded sweatshirt), and left my house decidedly. I was outside; the relief I felt was tremendous.

I began this book in the spring of 2004, but, for life, it took me four years to complete it. The writing of *Toaf* converges on the writing of *AF*, and suddenly there are ten years to the question. And a group of people who have been with me the whole time: Jen Hofer, Rachel Bernstein, Aja Duncan, and Rachel Levitsky. It is to them that I dedicate this book.

Atelos was founded in 1995 as a project of Hip's Road and is devoted to publishing, under the sign of poetry, writing that challenges the conventional definitions of poetry, since such definitions have tended to isolate poetry from intellectual life, arrest its development, and curtail its impact.

All the works published as part of the Atelos project are commissioned specifically for it, and each is involved in some way with crossing traditional genre boundaries, including for example, those that would separate theory from practice, poetry from prose, essay from drama, the visual image from the verbal, the literary from the non-literary, and so forth.

The Atelos project when complete will consist of 50 volumes.

The project directors and editors are Lyn Hejinian and Travis Ortiz. The director for text production and design is Travis Ortiz; the director for cover production and design is Ree Katrak / Great Bay Graphics.

Atelos (current volumes):

1. *The Literal World*, by Jean Day
2. *Bad History*, by Barrett Watten
3. *True*, by Rae Armantrout
4. *Pamela: A Novel*, by Pamela Lu
5. *Cable Factory 20*, by Lytle Shaw
6. *R-hu*, by Leslie Scalapino
7. *Verisimilitude*, by Hung Q. Tu
8. *Alien Tatters*, by Clark Coolidge
9. *Forthcoming*, by Jalal Toufic
10. *Gardener of Stars*, by Carla Harryman
11. *lighthouse*, by M. Mara-Ann
12. *Some Vague Wife*, by Kathy Lou Schultz
13. *The Crave*, by Kit Robinson
14. *Fashionable Noise: On Digital Poetics*, by Brian Kim Stefans

Distributed by:

Small Press Distribution
1341 Seventh Street
Berkeley, California
            94710-1403

Atelos
P. O. Box 5814
Berkeley, California
            94705-0814

to order from SPD call 510-524-1668 or toll-free 800-869-7553
fax orders to: 510-524-0852
order via e-mail: orders@spdbooks.org
order online: www.spdbooks.org

To After That
(Toaf)
was printed in an edition of 750 copies
at Thomson-Shore, Inc.
Text design and typesetting by Travis Ortiz
using American Typewriter and Garamond
Cover design by Ree Katrak